BE SALES**TOUGH**™

The **8 FUNDAMENTALS** to being
TOUGH IN SALES

SALES
TOUGH

STEP UP. WORK HARD. BE VALUABLE.

By Sam Parker & Jim Gould
Cofounders of JustSell.com

For those who move the world

CONTENTS

SALES**TOUGH**
salz-tuf, adj.

01/ Characterized by uncompromising determination

02/ Resilient

03/ Relentlessly prepared, objective & service-oriented

.

Are you SALES**TOUGH**?

Here's where it begins…

01/

Let nothing interrupt your **MONEY HOURS**… the hours in a salesday when one can talk with prospects and/ or customers.

(the most valuable hours in the day)

NOTHING INTERRUPTS THE MONEY HOURS

TODAY is 20% of your sales week.

Two salesdays are 10% of your month.

To have only two slow days each month is equivalent to having more than one full month of slow days each year.

SALES POINT...

Every moment of every salesday matters. These are your **MONEY HOURS**. Hesitation for a better salesday of the week or a time when you're feeling more up to the task will have a long-term effect on your ultimate sales results (and discipline).

IT'S THIS SERIOUS. Every salesday is a salesday, regardless of circumstances.

Once it's gone, it's gone forever.

Over the next few weeks, begin your quest for **COMPLETE SALESTIME DISCIPLINE** regardless of environment... regardless of circumstances. Put the "Do Not Disturb" button on your money hours and on your sales discipline.

Time management is simple. Do what it is you know **MUST BE DONE**.

Please visit justsell.com/moneyhours for printable **money hours reminders.**

"**DEFER NO TIME**, delays have dangerous ends."

WILLIAM SHAKESPEARE (1564-1616)
English playwright & poet

02/

Start **EARLY** and go **LONG**.

START EARLY AND GO LONG

Something important – **SOMETHING VERY IMPORTANT** – a thought on starting and finishing…

Three quick questions:

01/ Of the 20 or so salesdays each month, how many times do you start earlier than is expected of you?

02/ How many times do you work later than is expected of you?

03/ How many times are you early for an appointment?

Starting early and going long **COUNT**. Being prompt **MATTERS**. The impact on you in terms of how it's viewed by your executive team, management team, peers, subordinates, prospects, and customers can be tremendous – tremendously positive or tremendously negative.

On time – starting, leaving, or arriving – is simply what's expected.

To be early and go long sends a message of purpose, commitment, and respect – to others and yourself – and assures better results over time. To be even one minute late, or rarely be challenged ending your day on time, sends a completely different message.

Emerson suggested, "Activity is contagious."

Have an impact on everyone. Enjoy great results.

Embrace the early start. Go long.

Inspire yourself and others. Now.

"The way to get started is to quit talking and **BEGIN DOING**."

WALT DISNEY (1901-1966)
American entrepreneur, movie producer, showman

03/

Live a salesday schedule of **CALLS FIRST**, paperwork last.

CALLS FIRST, PAPERWORK LAST

AT WHAT TIME did you make your **FIRST SALES CALL** today? How about yesterday?

Remember, your salesday begins with the **FIRST CALL** you make to a prospect or customer. Prep activity, paperwork, and water cooler talk don't kick off a salesday.

Consider a schedule that **COMMITS** you and your team to making contact with prospects and customers at the first possible moment of the day and carries until your midday lunch break. Upon return, get right back to **MAKING CONTACT**. If paperwork, meetings, or other non-selling activities can't be done outside the money hours, save them for the final hour of the day. With this approach, you'll minimize the chance of your non-selling activities bloating into your **IRREPLACEABLE** selling time and stealing your would-be revenue (and commission) possibilities.

TAKE IT ONE STEP FURTHER.

Once you've finished your end-of-the-day activities, make one more call and create roughly 250 additional sales opportunities each year.

Top-level thinking (and action) only.

"The future depends entirely on what
EACH OF US DOES every day."

GLORIA STEINEM (1944-   )
American journalist, founder of Ms. Magazine

04/

Excite your prospects with
STRONG OPENING STATEMENTS
that mean something.

OPEN STRONG

Nothing is more important to prospecting (other than actually doing it) than the quality of your opening statement.

In person or over the phone, windows of attention are typically slammed shut in less than 10 seconds. This means you have to maximize the impact of every word, syllable, and pause in your lead-off statements. They need to be works of art – **COMPELLING** to the extreme degree. To minimize the importance of preparing a solid opening statement is to potentially short circuit your entire sales effort.

Fortunately, opening statements can be prepared and practiced **BEFORE** a sales opportunity is ever pursued.

REMEMBER, it's very likely the people you're trying to reach are also being approached by many others each day (competitors or not). A powerful, compelling, and practiced opening statement can launch many sales opportunities for you, where a competitor's lack of preparation can leave them standing still.

Your guide to creating effective opening statements begins on page 69 in the Sales Tools section.

"Life all comes down to a few moments. This is ONE OF THEM."

BUD FOX
Stockbroker from the film "Wall Street" (1987)

05/

KNOW EVERYONE (network more).

KNOW EVERYONE

Networking is about contact...

CONTACT WITH PEOPLE.

A primary business activity for those who drive revenue (and even those who think they don't*), networking is a skill set well worth developing. In fact, it's a **NECESSITY** for those striving to do something exceptional with their career. And, like all other parts of the sales process, it can be distilled into a few very primary fundamentals.

Sometime this year, you're sure to be in a networking environment (formal or informal). It may be a tradeshow, or an association or civic meeting. Or, you may find yourself at the national sales meeting with an opportunity to meet the home office people who make sure your customers are served well.

*Everyone drives revenue in one way or another.

If you have nothing on the radar at the moment, then see what networking opportunities you can create. There's immediate and long-term value to you and those with whom you connect.

It's **ASSURED**.

Your guide to successful networking begins on page 79 in the Sales Tools section.

"Unless you **LOVE EVERYBODY**, you can't sell anybody."

THE LATE DICKY FOX
The original sports agent
from the film, "Jerry Maguire" (1996)

06/

Develop a comfort with closing through **SOLID PREPARATION** and **SOLID FRONT WORK**.

CLOSE COMFORTABLY

Closing tends to be one of the most stressful actions in the sales process for so many people – salespeople and prospects.

Your responsibility as a sales professional is to work the earlier stages of the sales process so that closing becomes a **NATURAL CONCLUSION** if both parties benefit – this includes closing continually throughout the process. Keep in mind, closing is really the beginning of your business relationship – both parties should be excited about working together.

It's not about silver bullets. It's not about slick lines.

Closing comfort comes from basic preparation… done well.

Your guide to closing with confidence begins on page 91 in the Sales Tools section.

"Great things are not done by impulse, but by a SERIES OF SMALL THINGS brought together."

VINCENT VAN GOGH (1853 – 1890)
Dutch painter

07/

Keep any complaints or problems **TO YOURSELF** (**ESPECIALLY** when you're with prospects or customers).

SOLVE PROBLEMS, DON'T SHARE THEM

Be careful to keep your personal challenges to yourself during the salesday.

Eliminate anything that can potentially distract your customers and prospects from the benefits of your product or service (or from you building a positive business relationship).

This should be fairly easy, unless your prospects or customers begin sharing their personal challenges with you. At that point, you might have a tendency to join in. Remember to do what you can to minimize it. Empathize. Care about their situation. Help if you feel it's appropriate, but avoid matching your personal challenges with theirs.

During **SALESTIME**, you have no problems – you solve them.

It's all about them.

"When it's not always raining, there'll be days like this / When there's NO ONE COMPLAINING, there'll be days like this."

VAN MORRISON (1945 -   )
Irish-American music artist

08/

Pause at the beginning of each week or month to quickly (and objectively) evaluate your personal **SALES VALUE**.

YOUR PERSONAL SALES VALUE

ASK YOURSELF, DO YOUR ACTIONS…

01/ Create **A POSITIVE BUZZ** about you and your work?

02/ Make **OTHERS WANT YOU** as a part of their team?

03/ Make **YOUR EMPLOYER CRINGE** at the thought of losing you to a competitor?

04/ Make **YOUR CUSTOMERS EXCITED** about referring you to their colleagues?

You want your actions to **SCREAM VALUE** without the need for you to say a word. This is where you want to be – with those in your company and industry…and with those to whom you're selling.

This is what creates true economic and job security – the value you and your team create for others.

This is care.

When you have the opportunity over the next few days, set a reminder to review these four questions at the end of each month. Give yourself a little attention by creating an action plan to improve in each area where you feel you should.

Easier said than done... still needs to be done.

THE FUNDAMENTAL TRUTHS OF SALES VALUE

External value (among your prospects & customers)

01/ How well you and your product/service help them meet their perceived need

02/ The level to which your customers and prospects enjoy working with you

Internal value (within your company)

01/ Meeting and exceeding sales goals (dollars and units)

02/ Meeting and exceeding activity goals

03/ Your intangible contribution to your team (attitude-based: do others find you helpful, inspiring, a pleasure to work with, etc.)

04/ Your level of expertise on your own product/service and industry

"The people at the very top don't work just harder or even much harder than everyone else. They work MUCH, MUCH HARDER."

MALCOLM GLADWELL (1963 -   )
Canadian journalist

It's time to be SALES**TOUGH**™

Start with simple SALES**TOUGH**™ commitments…

01/ Let nothing interrupt your money hours (the hours in your day when you can talk with your prospects or customers). If you're a leader, commit your money hours to your people.

02/ Start early and go long every day. Just 15 minutes more at the beginning and end of each day adds 10 money hours to your month (more than a full salesday)… and more than two extra sales weeks a year.

03/ Commit to attending at least three networking events each quarter – one event per month. Make contact with just a couple new people at each event, and in one year, you'll add 25 new people who might positively impact your sales world.

04/ Complain less, just once daily, and choke off 5 seeds of negativity for the sales week.

Sales **TOOLS**

CREATING YOUR OPENING STATEMENT

Nothing is more important to prospecting (other than actually doing it) than the quality of your opening statement.

Fortunately, opening statements can be prepared and practiced before a sales opportunity is ever pursued. Here are some guidelines and thoughts for creating your opening statement(s), as well as some samples for you to rework into your sales world.

THE OBJECTIVE: Create immediate interest for further discussion… engage the prospect.

THE METHOD: Work through the following questions and tips using pen to paper or fingers to keyboard.

What do I sell?

Answer this using as few words as possible. Avoid using words or phrases that mean nothing to outsiders (e.g., industry acronyms, fluffy corporate communications language, etc.).

How do my customers benefit when they buy my product/service?

If you sell to consumers, include the potential added emotional benefits of being liked, respected, more attractive, etc., if these benefits exist. If you sell to businesses, be sure to include the emotional benefits to the purchasing customer (the decision maker) in addition to the more specific benefits realized by the company (a good buy or product implementation can be the road to promotion or status within an organization). You're looking for several true benefits, not simply features.

//

Now...

Build several opening statements for the different scenarios you might face (e.g., catching a decision maker without a screener or gatekeeper, catching a decision maker "on the way out the door," delivering the opening statement to a screener who insists on knowing "what's this in reference to?," leaving a voice mail, etc.).

Address each of the following in whatever order seems most appropriate for your particular sales world (just make sure the benefit to your prospect is mentioned within the first 10 seconds):

- Who you are
- Where you're from (company name)
- What you sell (in very simple terms)
- How your prospect will benefit from your product or service
- A question to gauge the interest level of the prospect

//

Keep in mind...

- Opening statements aren't meant to close a prospect... they're meant to get attention and engage someone.
- Maximize every word, syllable, and pause.
- Never leave a misleading or vague voice mail message – hit them with your complete and prepared opening (it should be short enough)... if it was worth dialing the phone, it's worth leaving your opening statement... you will not trick someone into buying something because you "caught them."
- Never use industry jargon or unnecessary thousand dollar words.
- Avoid being vague.

Consider using words like…

- Maximize, increase, grow [sales, customer retention, productivity, etc.]
- Minimize, reduce, decrease, eliminate [expenses, customer service challenges, diversions, etc.]
- Profit from
- Specific, specifically
- Save, conserve
- Accumulate, acquire
- Prevent
- Fully
- Immediate, now

Avoid using phrases like...

- How are you today?
- I'd like to learn more about your business to determine...
- We're the leading provider of...
- We work with several of your competitors...
- I'd like to see if there are some ways we might work together.
- Is now a good time to talk?
- Did I catch you at a bad time?

These phrases may be used at other times during the sales process, but they have no place in the opening statement because they don't capture immediate attention or encourage the prospect to engage with you, and therefore, can take away from the initial attention allotted to you by the prospect.

Sample opening statements

Hi, [first name]. We provide [product/service] in order to help people [take advantage of, minimize, maximize, prevent, etc.] [something of importance]. I'm calling to see if this might be helpful to [you/your clients].

Hi, [first name]. [your name] with [company name]. We help companies fully profit from their existing resources through our [product/service] that [does/has/have whatever differentiating point or feature]. I'm calling to see if you'd be interested in discussing how it might help your [whatever] efforts/initiatives.

Hi, [first name]. [your name], [company name]. We deliver [product/service] which might be able to save you more than [specific percentage] on your [whatever] expenses. Would you be interested in discussing how it might fit into your environment?

"The **MOST VALUABLE** of all talents ... that of never using two words where one will do."

THOMAS JEFFERSON (1743 – 1826)
Third president of the United States
Principal author of the Declaration of Independence

(JustSell)

THE NETWORKING GUIDE

This is your guide to the fundamentals of successful networking…Just Sell® style.

Work it. Practice it. Improve it. And work the room.

Finesse points are developed with experience, **BY
DOING**. Nail these fundamentals and you'll make
every networking experience you'll ever have a
pleasure for you and for everyone with whom you
connect – professionally and personally.

It's your time. It's your event. It's your room.

//

Well before the event...

With your particular event and its attendees in mind, prepare (in writing) and practice (verbally delivering)...

YOUR QUICK PERSONAL INTRODUCTION

- Appropriate to the event
- Nothing fancy, no value statement here
- Use the person's name if you know it or if they're wearing a name tag

SAMPLE...

"Hi, Susan. I'm Bob Jones [with XYZ company, in District 7, in the forms division]"

//

//

GENERAL STATEMENTS/QUESTIONS THAT WILL HELP INITIATE A CONVERSATION

(Be prepared with at least 3)

- How long have you been [a member of, involved with] [specific group]?
- What brought you out here [today, tonight]?
- Have you been to a [meeting type] before?
- What do you think of the [show, meeting, event, etc.] so far?
- What did you think of the last [show, meeting, event, etc.]?
- What do you think about [event-specific thing or event]?
- How do you know [speaker, organizer of the event, sponsoring group of the event]?

//

OPEN-ENDED QUESTIONS

(Be prepared with at least 3)

- Choose your favorites with the particular event in mind.
- Use the open-ended questions (page 99 of the Sales Tools section) or create some of your own.

YOUR VALUE STATEMENTS

(Be prepared with at least 2)

- Statements of what you sell/do in terms of the value it delivers to others
- You may never have an appropriate time to deliver these (over-the-top selling in a networking setting can turn people off), just be prepared.

//

EXIT STATEMENTS

(Be prepared with at least 1 of each kind)

Statement for scheduled follow up:

- Can I give you a call next week to set up a time to talk in more detail?

- Would you like to get together on Friday and work through the idea?

Statement for exit with no follow up:

- Good meeting you. Will I see you at [other meetings, events, etc.]?

- Well that sounds exciting. Best of luck with that. I'll let you get back to [whatever the person was doing prior to talking with you]. Enjoyed meeting you.

- It's quite an event. We should probably keep moving. I enjoyed talking with you, Bob.

//

//

Just before the event...

SET CLEAR OBJECTIVES AND GOALS

- Specific people with whom you want to meet or talk
- Quantity of discussions you want to have
- Number of post-event meetings or phone calls you want to schedule

PREPARE YOUR ATTITUDE

- Completely positive (no "tradeshow cynicism")
- Inquisitive, pleasant, and service-oriented mindset

//

At the event...

To fully maximize your time at an event and stay on course, it's helpful to keep in mind that you are to...

01/ **APPROACH** people proactively (and be approach-able to others).

02/ **ENGAGE** them.

03/ **LEARN** about them, and when appropriate, **INFORM** them about you, your company/product/service.

04/ **EXIT** and move on.

Then, work toward your objectives and goals by...

PROACTIVELY INITIATING DISCUSSIONS

- Use your prepared and practiced introductions and initiating statements.

SENDING THE RIGHT MESSAGE PHYSICALLY

- Face the person completely.
- Smile.
- Show energy.

ASKING OPEN-ENDED QUESTIONS

- Listen completely (without the intent to respond immediately or show your knowledge).
- Allow small gaps of silence (in many cases, the other person will fill them with more information – sometimes extra information that's useful).

GIVING UNDIVIDED ATTENTION TO THE PERSON IN FRONT OF YOU

- Avoid wandering and scanning eyes (your goal is one-on-one attention).
- Delay giving any attention to a cell phone or other personal device until you're no longer engaged in the conversation.

DELIVERING YOUR VALUE STATEMENTS

- Only when it feels right (avoid pushy).

MAINTAINING YOUR NETWORKING ATTITUDE THROUGH THE END OF THE EVENT

- Complete positive follow through (it's showtime, literally... use it well)
- Rest **AFTER** the event.

//

After the event...

QUICKLY EVALUATE YOUR PERFORMANCE

- Review against your objectives and goals for the event and indentify where you might improve.

FOLLOW UP WITH APPROPRIATE INDIVIDUALS

- Written form as soon as possible (handwritten note, letter, or email)
- Call for a more personal connection

SEEK OUT YOUR NEXT EVENT

- Set a target (once a month, quarter, etc.).
- Join a networking or lead referral club.
- Consider attending one or two networking events a year in other industries to stretch your thinking and relationship possibilities.

//

"Let no one ever come to you without leaving BETTER and HAPPIER."

MOTHER TERESA (1910-1997)
Albanian missionary
Nobel Peace Prize winner

THE CLOSING CHECKLIST

The closing tool is designed to give you and your team a quick and comprehensive checklist of your "need-to-know" points before attempting a standard close (trial closes don't require the knowledge of all "need-to-know" points – trial closes serve as more of a qualifying function and help the process move to the standard close).

While it may be valuable to have a basic understanding of the "traditional" closes articulated in many older sales manuals (e.g., the assumptive, the puppy dog, the physical action, the choice, the last chance, etc.), it's these "need-to-know" points that create the opportunity for any effective close – these are non-manipulative and universal.

The correct answers to the following questions assist in developing the close into the natural conclusion we all seek in the process. Work through them for each prospect in your pipeline right now and be sure you're on the right track to closure.

//

Additionally, some sample closing statements are included. These are simple statements and questions that help everyone involved in the sales process move smoothly to closure. Use what you like, toss what you don't, and build upon those most appropriate for your sales world.

THE CLOSING CHECKLIST

01/ Is there value in my product for my prospect?

02/ What is the hard-dollar value? (return on investment, money savings, etc.)

03/ What other value is there? (prestige, safety, non-monetary improvements, etc.)

04/ Does the prospect understand and value the benefits of my product or service?

05/ Is a decision to buy my offering better than a decision to create it in-house (on their own)?

//

//

06/ What risks to the prospect do I need to minimize or alleviate in regard to this buying decision? (financial, time of implementation, opportunity cost, prestige, what their boss/peers might think, etc.)

07/ What urgency have I created to encourage the prospect to move forward now? (time to market, discounts, delivery incentives, guarantees, etc.)

08/ Why is buying my product or service a better decision than moving forward with my competitor (or taking no action at all)?

//

///

SAMPLE CLOSING STATEMENTS

To be most effective and minimize closing stress for everyone involved, closing statements should be practiced and delivered/asked with confidence and a positively expectant attitude.

- Would you like to move forward?
- Are you ready to get started?
- Can we go ahead?
- We can start the process today with a credit card, if you'd like.
- We can deliver it to you by the close of business tomorrow, if you'd like.
- We can have it delivered by the end of the month if we can get a signed contract into the implementation department by Thursday.
- Should I forward a contract so you can get started?
- Would you like to try it for a quarter?
- It'll take a few weeks to process and ship the order, so if you're interested in moving forward, we should start the paperwork now.

///

- Let's get this off your plate and start the paperwork. What do you think?
- Let's start the process so you can get onto your other priorities. Sound good?

///

"There will come a time when you believe everything is finished. That will be THE BEGINNING."

LOUIS L'AMOUR (1908 - 1988)
American writer

///

THE OPEN-ENDED QUESTIONS

Open-ended questions are one of the most valuable tools for those who sell (as long as you listen). They help gather information, qualify sales opportunities, and establish rapport, trust, and credibility. With such **CORE IMPORTANCE** to the sales process, **THE PROFESSIONAL** leaves little to chance when it comes to owning a repertoire of powerful open-ended questions… questions that are answered by more than a simple yes or no… questions where the prospect or customer gets directly involved in the sales discussion.

THE KEY HERE…

Ask the question and let the prospect or customer give you their answer.

NO LEADING.
NO PROMPTING.
NO INTERRUPTING.

///

In case you've not had the opportunity to put yours **IN WRITING**, here are some of our favorites (you'll likely have several additional questions specific to your industry, but these'll get you more than started).

The open-ended questions...

INFORMATION GATHERING QUESTIONS

- What prompted you/your organization to look into this?
- What are your expectations/requirements for this product/service?
- What process did you go through to determine your needs?
- How do you see this happening?
- What is it that you'd like to see accomplished?
- With whom have you had success in the past?
- With whom have you had difficulties in the past?
- Can you help me understand that a little better?
- What does that mean?
- How does that process work now?
- What challenges does that process create?
- What challenges has that created in the past?
- What are the best things about that process?
- What other items should we discuss?

QUALIFYING QUESTIONS

- What do you see as the next action steps?
- What is your timeline for implementing/purchasing this type of service/product?
- What other data points should we know before moving forward?
- What budget has been established for this?
- What are your thoughts?
- Who else is involved in this decision?
- What could make this no longer a priority?
- What's changed since we last talked?
- What concerns do you have?

//

FOR ESTABLISHING RAPPORT, TRUST, & CREDIBILITY

- How did you get involved in...?
- What kind of challenges are you facing?
- What's the most important priority to you with this? Why?
- What other issues are important to you?
- What would you like to see improved?
- How do you measure that?

Write down the ones you find valuable. Commit them to memory with your team. Practice them on your drive in or on the way to your next appointment. Print them out. Tack them up near your phone. Pass them on to your sales team.

It's all about sales®.

Visit justsell.com/questions for a printable chart of these questions.

//

"If you're going to help a man, you want to **KNOW SOMETHING** about him, don't you?"

JOSEPH TO CLARENCE, ANGEL SECOND CLASS
From the film "It's a Wonderful Life" (1946)

A **MESSAGE** to Garcia

By Elbert Hubbard (1914)

"If I worked for a man... I would give an UNDIVIDED SERVICE."

ELBERT HUBBARD (1856-1915)
American businessman and writer

A MESSAGE TO GARCIA

In February 1899, in one hour after dinner, Elbert Hubbard wrote a 1500-word essay titled "A Message to Garcia."

A true story of responsibility and initiative, the piece went on to be printed more than 40 million times during the author's lifetime.

Hubbard's first sales job… selling soap.

The version that follows was produced in 1914 after the material had significant publishing success – it includes an introduction by the author and some additional closing thoughts.

For a free downloadable kid's version and other fun material, visit JustSell.com/Garcia. If you're a collector, you can occasionally find original copies auctioned on eBay.com. To learn more about Hubbard, PBS has a great documentary you can watch online at pbs.org/elbert-hubbard.

Apologia

HORSE SENSE

If you work for a man, in Heaven's name work for him. If he pays wages that supply you your bread and butter, work for him, speak well of him, think well of him, and stand by him, and stand by the institution he represents. I think if I worked for a man, I would work for him. I would not work for him a part of his time, but all of his time. I would give an undivided service or none. If put to the pinch, an ounce of loyalty is worth a pound of cleverness. If you must vilify, condemn, and eternally disparage, why, resign your position, and when you are outside, damn to your heart's content. But, I pray you, so long as you are a part of an institution, do not condemn it. Not that you will injure the institution – not that – but when you disparage the concern of which you are a part, you disparage yourself.

And don't forget – "I forgot" won't do in business.

This literary trifle, "A Message to Garcia," was written one evening after supper, in a single hour. It was on the Twenty-second of February, Eighteen Hundred Ninety-nine, Washington's Birthday, and we were just going to press with the March "Philistine." The thing leaped hot from my heart, written after a trying day, when I had been endeavoring to train some rather delinquent villagers to abjure the comatose state and get radio-active.

The immediate suggestion, though, came from a little argument over the teacups, when my boy Bert suggested that Rowan was the real hero of the Cuban War. Rowan had gone alone and done the thing – carried the message to Garcia.

It came to me like a flash! Yes, the boy is right, the hero is the man who does his work – who carries the message to Garcia. I got up from the table, and wrote "A Message to Garcia." I thought so little of it that we ran it in the Magazine without a heading. The edition went out, and soon orders began to come for extra copies of the March "Philistine," a dozen, fifty, a hundred; and when the American News Company ordered a thousand, I asked one of my helpers which article it was that had stirred up the cosmic dust.

"It's the stuff about Garcia," he said.

The next day a telegram came from George H. Daniels, of the New York Central Railroad, thus: "Give price on one hundred thousand Rowan article in pamphlet form – Empire State Express advertisement on back – also how soon can ship."

I replied giving price, and stated we could supply the pamphlets in two years. Our facilities were small and a hundred thousand booklets looked like an awful undertaking.

The result was that I gave Mr. Daniels permission to reprint the article in his own way. He issued it in booklet form in editions of half a million. Two or three of these half-million lots were sent out by Mr. Daniels, and in addition the article was reprinted in over two hundred magazines and newspapers. It has been translated into all written languages.

At the time Mr. Daniels was distributing the "Message to Garcia," Prince Hilakoff, Director of Russian Railways, was in this country. He was the guest of the New York Central, and made a tour of the country under the personal direction of Mr. Daniels. The Prince saw the little book and was interested in it, more because Mr. Daniels was putting it out in such big numbers, probably, than otherwise.

In any event, when he got home he had the matter translated into Russian, and a copy of the booklet given to every railroad employee in Russia.

Other countries then took it up, and from Russia it passed into Germany, France, Spain, Turkey, Hindustan and China. During the war between Russia and Japan, every Russian soldier who went to the front was given a copy of the "Message to Garcia."

The Japanese, finding the booklets in possession of the Russian prisoners, concluded that it must be a good thing, and accordingly translated it into Japanese.

And on an order of the Mikado, a copy was given to every man in the employ of the Japanese Government, soldier or civilian. Over forty million copies of "A Message to Garcia" have been printed.

This is said to be a larger circulation than any other literary venture has ever attained during the lifetime of the author, in all history – thanks to a series of lucky accidents!

E.H.

As the cold of snow in the time of harvest,
so is a faithful messenger to them that send him:
for he refresheth the soul of his masters.

Proverbs XXV: 13

A Message to Garcia

IN ALL THIS Cuban business there is one man stands out on the horizon of my memory like Mars at perihelion.

When war broke out between Spain and the United States, it was very necessary to communicate quickly with the leader of the Insurgents. Garcia was somewhere in the mountain fastnesses of Cuba – no one knew where. No mail or telegraph message could reach him. The President must secure his co-operation, and quickly. What to do!

Some one said to the President, "There is a fellow by the name of Rowan will find Garcia for you, if anybody can."

Rowan was sent for and was given a letter to be delivered to Garcia. How "the fellow by the name of Rowan" took the letter, sealed it up in an oilskin pouch, strapped it over his heart, in four days landed by night off the coast of Cuba from an open boat, disappeared into the jungle, and in three weeks came out on the other side of the Island, having traversed a hostile country on foot, and delivered his letter to Garcia – are things I have no special desire now to tell in detail. The point that I wish to make is this: McKinley gave Rowan a letter to be delivered to Garcia; Rowan took the letter and did not ask, "Where is he at?" By the Eternal! there is a man whose form should be cast in deathless bronze and the statue placed in every college of the land. It is not book-learning young men need, nor instruction about this and that, but **A STIFFENING OF THE VERTEBRAE** which will cause them to be loyal to a trust, to act promptly, concentrate their energies: do the thing – "Carry a message to Garcia."

General Garcia is dead now, but there are other Garcias.

No man who has endeavored to carry out an enterprise where many hands were needed, but has been well-nigh appalled at times by the imbecility of the average man – the inability or unwillingness to concentrate on a thing and do it.

Slipshod assistance, foolish inattention, dowdy indifference, and half-hearted work seem the rule; and no man succeeds, unless by hook or crook or threat he forces or bribes other men to assist him; or mayhap, God in His goodness performs a miracle, and sends him an Angel of Light for an assistant. You, reader, put this matter to a test: You are sitting now in your office – six clerks are within call. Summon any one and make this request: "Please look in the encyclopedia and make a brief memorandum for me concerning the life of Correggio."

Will the clerk quietly say, "Yes, sir," and go do the task?

On your life he will not. He will look at you out of a fishy eye and ask one or more of the following questions:

Who was he?

Which encyclopedia?

Where is the encyclopedia?

Was I hired for that?

Don't you mean Bismarck?

What's the matter with Charlie doing it?

Is he dead?

Is there any hurry?

Shall I bring you the book and let you look it up yourself?

What do you want to know for?

And I will lay you ten to one that after you have answered the questions, and explained how to find the information, and why you want it, the clerk will go off and get one of the other clerks to help him try to find Garcia – and then come back and tell you there is no such man. Of course I may lose my bet, but according to the Law of Average I will not.

Now, if you are wise, you will not bother to explain to your "assistant" that Correggio is indexed under the C's, not in the K's, but you will smile very sweetly and say, "Never mind," and go look it up yourself.

And this incapacity for independent action, this moral stupidity, this infirmity of the will, this unwillingness to cheerfully catch hold and lift – these are the things that put pure Socialism so far into the future. If men will not act for themselves, what will they do when the benefit of their effort is for all? A first mate with knotted club seems necessary; and the dread of getting "the bounce" Saturday night holds many a worker to his place.

Advertise for a stenographer, and nine out of ten who apply can neither spell nor punctuate – and do not think it necessary to.

Can such a one write a letter to Garcia?

"You see that bookkeeper," said a foreman to me in a large factory.

"Yes; what about him?"

"Well, he's a fine accountant, but if I'd send him up-town on an errand, he might accomplish the errand all right, and on the other hand, might stop at four saloons on the way, and when he got to Main Street would forget what he had been sent for."

Can such a man be entrusted to carry a message to Garcia?

We have recently been hearing much maudlin sympathy expressed for the "downtrodden denizens of the sweat-shop" and the "homeless wanderer searching for honest employment," and with it all often go many hard words for the men in power.

Nothing is said about the employer who grows old before his time in a vain attempt to get frowsy ne'er-do-wells to do intelligent work; and his long, patient striving with "help" that does nothing but loaf when his back is turned. In every store and factory there is a constant weeding-out process going on. The employer is continually sending away "help" that have shown their incapacity to further the interests of the business, and others are being taken on.

No matter how good times are, this sorting continues: only if times are hard and work is scarce, the sorting is done finer – but out and forever out the incompetent and unworthy go. It is the survival of the fittest. Self-interest prompts every employer to keep the best – those who can carry a message to Garcia.

I know one man of really brilliant parts who has not the ability to manage a business of his own, and yet who is absolutely worthless to any one else, because he carries with him constantly the insane suspicion that his employer is oppressing, or intending to oppress, him. He can not give orders; and he will not receive them. Should a message be given him to take to Garcia, his answer would probably be, "Take it yourself!"

Tonight this man walks the streets looking for work, the wind whistling through his threadbare coat. No one who knows him dare employ him, for he is a regular firebrand of discontent. He is impervious to reason, and the only thing that can impress him is the toe of a thick-soled Number Nine boot.

Of course I know that one so morally deformed is no less to be pitied than a physical cripple; but in our pitying let us drop a tear, too, for the men who are striving to carry on a great enterprise, whose **WORKING HOURS ARE NOT LIMITED BY THE WHISTLE**, and whose hair is fast turning white through the struggle to hold in line dowdy indifference, slipshod imbecility, and the heartless ingratitude which, but for their enterprise, would be both hungry and homeless.

Have I put the matter too strongly? Possibly I have; but when all the world has gone a-slumming I wish to speak a word of sympathy for the man who succeeds – the man who, against great odds, has directed the efforts of others, and having succeeded, finds there's nothing in it: nothing but bare board and clothes. I have carried a dinner-pail and worked for day's wages, and I have also been an employer of labor, and I know there is something to be said on both sides. There is no excellence, per se, in poverty; rags are no recommendation; and all employers are not rapacious and high-handed, any more than all poor men are virtuous.

My heart goes out to the man who does his work when the "boss" is away, as well as when he is at home. And the man who, when given a letter for Garcia, quietly takes the missive, without asking any idiotic questions, and with no lurking intention of chucking it into the nearest sewer, or of doing aught else but deliver it, never gets "laid off," nor has to go on a strike for higher wages. Civilization is one long, anxious search for just such individuals. Anything such a man asks shall be granted. His kind is so rare that no employer can afford to let him go. He is wanted in every city, town and village – in every office, shop, store and factory.

The world cries out for such: he is needed, and needed badly – the man who can carry a message to Garcia.

To act in absolute freedom and at the same time know that responsibility is the price of freedom is salvation.

Life in Abundance

The supreme prayer of my heart is not to be learned or "good," but to be Radiant.

I desire to radiate health, cheerfulness, sincerity, calm courage and good-will.

I wish to be simple, honest, natural, frank, clean in mind and clean in body, unaffected – ready to say, "I do not know," if so it be, to meet all men on an absolute equality – face any obstacle and meet every difficulty unafraid and unabashed.

I wish others to live their lives, too, up to their highest, fullest and best. To that end I pray that I may never meddle, dictate, interfere, give advice that is not wanted, nor assist when my services are not needed. If I can help people I'll do it by giving them a chance to help themselves; and if I can uplift or inspire, let it be by example, inference and suggestion, rather than by injunction and dictation. That is to say, I desire to be Radiant – to Radiate Life.

About the Authors

SAM PARKER

Sam co-founded Give More Media Inc. (publishers of JustSell.com) in early 1998 after selling for more than a decade in several different industries – financial services, pharmaceuticals, joint replacements, office products, and software. Today, he continues his role in serving the subscribers of JustSell.com and its sponsoring partners.

He's also the author of 212° the extra degree® and Smile & Move™, blogs at JustParker.com, occasionally speaks to groups, has a degree in marketing from James Madison University (1987), and sells daily.

He frequently thanks Jim for being the master of business administration so he doesn't have to.

"Work in a way that makes your employer continually think of WAYS to keep you rather than REASONS to keep you."

SAM PARKER (1965 -   )
Co-founder JustSell.com

About the Authors

JIM GOULD

Jim co-founded Give More Media Inc. Before Give More, he was in sales and management for an international finance company and in 1997, caught the web bug with an Internet banking company (before online banking actually used the web).

Jim guest lectures to university classes on entrepreneurship, sales, and online marketing. He graduated from James Madison University (1988) with degrees in finance and international business, and from George Mason University (1997) with a master in business administration.

He secretly wishes Sam would have become a master in business administration as well.

About JustSell.com

JustSell.com is a free resource for sales executives, managers, and professionals. Its email newsletters and site provide professional development tips and ideas to help inspire great sales results...pure sales love™.

Your professional life is half of who you are – half of the value you create. It welcomes your attention... and deserves it.

Sales is serious. Without it, nothing else exists.

To join over 100,000 subscribers of Just Sell's free email newsletters, please visit JustSell.com.

The Just Sell® team is located in Richmond, Virginia. They can be reached at 804-762-4500.

Also by Sam Parker

212° the extra degree®

At 211 degrees, water is hot. At 212 degrees, it boils.
And with boiling water, comes steam.
And with steam, **you can power a train**.

Just one extra degree can make all the difference.

212° the extra degree® is an inspiring message with
a singular focus on effort. It illustrates how small
things can have a big impact on results.

The book and material have been purchased and/or
licensed by people at Nike, Wal-Mart, Gap, Verizon,
Hershey, Disney, McDonald's, New York Life,
NASCAR, U.S. Olympic Committee, Marriott, Ernst
& Young, Bank of America, hundreds of schools,
and many others.

To enjoy the 3.5 minute 212 video, please
visit… **Just212.com/be212**.

Also by Sam Parker

Smile & Move®

"Write it on your heart that every day is the best day in the year."

Ralph Waldo Emerson (1803-1882)
American writer and activist

Sam's follow-up message to 212 gives us a reminder to happily serve… to "Smove."

It's all about attitude and action. Being positive and having a sense of urgency. Having effect. Mattering to the world, all with a smile.

Enjoy the 3-minute Smile & Move video and join the Smovement by visiting **SmileAndMove.com/rockit**.

Smovers are everywhere. Some of our bigger customers are people at Comcast, Tiffany, Disney, Hilton, Target, State Farm Insurance, Gap, two branches of the U.S. military, and several school and healthcare systems.

Gratitude

Everything we learn begins from the work of other people. **Thank you**…

World changers, writers, teachers, speakers, and philosophers who inspired and continue to inspire us: Jesus, Gandhi, Teresa, King, Adams, Franklin, Lincoln, Roosevelts, Churchill, Emerson, Frankl, Edison, Einstein, Disney, Jobs, Gates, Branson, Winfrey, Stewart, Ash, Wise, Pickford, Ball, Presley, Cash, Lennon, McCartney, Jagger, Springsteen, Lucas, Coppola, Spielberg, Hubbard, Carnegie, Peters, Covey, Rohn, Ziglar, Blanchard, Maxwell, Tracy, Gitomer, Gschwandtner, Godin, Lewis, Coelho, Collins, Gladwell, Livingston, Hanh, and so many more.

Mentors & managers: Lee, Otto & Jeanne, Rich, Jim, and Christophe.

The JustSell team (those with us and those who've gone on to kick@ss elsewhere) and JustSell subscribers.

Prospects and customers for the experience (and the opportunities).

To order SALES**TOUGH**

Sales**Tough**™ is available through Give More Media.

To purchase Sales**Tough**™ books and training materials, 212° the extra degree®, and Smile & Move™ (also by Sam Parker), please visit GiveMore.com or call 866-952-4483.

For free printable reminders and Sales**Tough**™ computer wallpapers, visit SalesTough.com.

STEP UP. WORK HARD. **BE VALUABLE.**™